Mollie MAKES

WEDDINGS

♥making ♥thrifting ♥collecting ♥crafting

CONTENTS

HANDMADE
INVITES

BOUQUETS
AND FLOWERS

WEDDING FAVORS

TABLE DECORATIONS

YOUR BIG DAY

It's the biggest day of your life, and the perfect opportunity to design a party that reflects the two of you! As well as ensuring you get the look you're after, making your nuptials handmade is a great excuse to invite friends and family along before the shindig for some fun craft-alongs. Put loved ones to work on Kirsty Neale's chalkboard feather napkin rings for your place settings or her 3D diamond garland – a pretty backdrop to summer garden weddings or indoor affairs alike.

We have brought together 20 projects for this compendium of big day ideas from all our favorite Mollie Makes designers. Combining crochet, paper, fabric, embellishments, felt, clay, and cross stitch, there's a huge range of techniques here to try your hand at. Create everything from Ilaria Chiaratti's glass-painted flower displays to Gretel Parker's gorgeous needlefelted polar bear cake toppers.

With clear instructions as well as projects for beginners and experienced crafters, we're sure you'll find something to inspire the most special of occasions. Enjoy!

Lots of love and congratulations from the Mollie Makes team,

Lara

Lara Watson
Editor, *Mollie Makes*

STITCHED PAPER
SAVE-THE-DAY GARLAND

ONCE THE WEDDING DATE HAS BEEN SET, YOU'LL BE KEEN TO LET FRIENDS AND FAMILY KNOW SO THEY CAN BE SURE TO SAVE THE DAY. THIS QUICK-TO-MAKE GARLAND CAN BE HUNG TO REMIND YOUR GUESTS OF THE FORTHCOMING EVENT LONG BEFORE THE FORMAL INVITES ARE SENT OUT. IT CONCERTINA-FOLDS INTO ENVELOPE SLEEVES FOR EASE OF POSTING.

DATE REMINDER

HOW TO MAKE ... SAVE-THE-DAY GARLAND

MATERIALS

THIN CARD STOCK IN COLORS OF YOUR CHOOSING FOR THE ENVELOPE SLEEVES

SELECTION OF PATTERNED PAPERS FOR THE DATE PENNANTS

TRACING PAPER

NARROW RIBBON

NUMBER AND LETTER STAMPS

INK PAD

CUTTING MAT, CRAFT KNIFE, AND METAL RULER

SEWING MACHINE

TIP
To create a vintage-style garland, recycle scraps of wrapping paper, postcards, letters, and photographs, and look out for wood-block stamps at yard sales.

01 For the envelope sleeves, cut out two rectangles of thin card stock, one measuring approx 9" x 7" (23 x 18 cm) and the other measuring approx 8" x 6" (20.5 x 15 cm). Fold each in half widthways.

02 For the date pennant backgrounds, cut out rectangles from your patterned paper selection, each measuring approx 3⅛" x 4½" (8 x 11.5 cm)—one for each number of the date, plus two to use as dividers between the date elements.

03 Cut out rectangles of tracing paper to the exact same size as the patterned paper rectangles. Print each number of the date onto the tracing paper rectangles, and print a decorative motif, such as a small starburst or a heart, for the date dividers. A selection of different typefaces has been used to print the date on our garland, but this is not essential. Pair each of the tracing paper overlays with a patterned paper background to complete the date pennants.

04 Now attach the date pennants to the ribbon. To make sure you cut the ribbon to the right length, lay the date pennants along the ribbon, positioning them with a ⅝" (1.5 cm) space in between and extending twice the width of the envelope sleeve plus 1½" (3.8 cm) at each side. Make sure you have the date in the correct order, then machine stitch the date pennants to the ribbon length.

CLARE YOUNGS

Designer-maker Clare was given a craft book with a pile of paper and fabric at the age of eight, and she hasn't stopped making since! Having trained as a graphic designer, she worked in packaging and illustration until turning to craft full time. Clare has written several craft books. To find out more, visit www.clareyoungs.co.uk

05 At the left-hand side of the garland, place 1½" (3.8 cm) of the ribbon inside the top edge of the larger of the card envelope sleeves, aligning the top of the ribbon to the edge of the card. Machine stitch close to the top edge of the folded card to secure the ribbon in place. Repeat to attach the ribbon to the smaller of the card envelope sleeves on the right-hand side of the garland (see photo). Machine stitch both envelope sleeves along the bottom edge.

06 Using a small coin as a guide, draw a semicircle halfway down the open-ended edge of the larger envelope sleeve, and cut out.

07 Decorate the front of the envelope sleeves with the bride and groom's initials. Add a decorative motif to the larger envelope sleeve (here we used a printed heart). Concertina-fold the date pennants together and place them into the smaller (right-hand) envelope sleeve. Slip the smaller envelope sleeve into the larger (left-hand) sleeve.

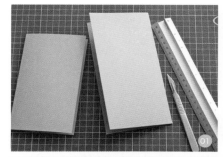

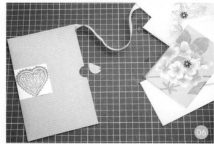

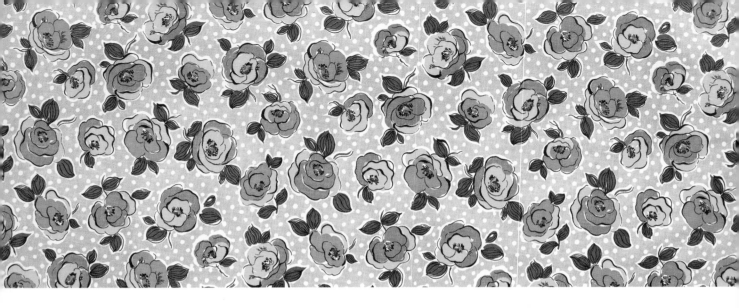

BUTTON STEM
BRIDAL BOUQUET

USE VINTAGE AND MODERN BUTTONS TO CREATE A RAINBOW-COLORED WEDDING BOUQUET. INDIVIDUAL "FLOWER" STEMS ARE MADE FROM STACKED BUTTONS, WHICH ARE THEN GATHERED TOGETHER TO MAKE A SIMPLE YET STUNNING POSY MEASURING ABOUT 8" (20.5 CM) HIGH x 6" (15 CM) WIDE FOR A LASTING WEDDING DAY MEMENTO.

EVERLASTING
FLOWERS

HOW TO MAKE ... BRIDAL BOUQUET

MATERIALS

ABOUT 250 BUTTONS

70 PIECES OF GREEN FLORAL WIRE
EACH MEASURING ABOUT 12" (30.5 CM)

1⅛ YARDS (1 M) OF 1" (2.5 CM) WIDE GREEN
GROSGRAIN RIBBON

GREEN FLORAL TAPE

PAIR OF PLIERS

FABRIC GLUE

TIP

Source buttons from craft fairs,
sewing supply stores, and
vintage markets. Or ask your
grandma if you can raid her
button tin.

01 Gather together a large collection of rainbow-colored buttons. You should choose as wide a variety as you can, from solid plastic to translucent glass. Try to find some buttons that have interesting textures or novelty shapes. You will need a good selection of buttons in terms of their size and shape.

02 Start to stack your buttons together to give interesting color combinations, making sure to place the smallest buttons on the top of each stack. Use two, three, or four buttons for each button flower. You will need about 70 button stacks, and do try to make these as varied as possible.

03 Take a piece of the floral wire and fold it in half to make a loop. Thread one of your button stacks onto the wire loop. Hold the wire firmly as you thread the buttons all the way to the end of the loop.

04 Twist the wire to hold the buttons firmly in place, using pliers to tighten if necessary. Continue to thread each button stack onto each piece of floral wire to make a total of 70

button flower stems. For the neatest finish, wrap each individual stem with green floral tape to hide the twisted wires. This has the added advantage of making the stems stronger so that they are less prone to bend out of shape.

05 Now begin to arrange the button flower stems together to make your bouquet, adding each stem one at a time and checking the shape of the bouquet as you go. Make sure you place contrasting buttons next to each other to add interest.

06 Once you are happy with the bouquet's shape, secure the stems together with floral tape to form the bouquet handle. Take the green ribbon and, starting at the bottom of the stems, begin to wrap the ribbon around the handle. If necessary you can secure the ribbon in place as you go with fabric glue. When you reach the top of the handle, trim off any excess ribbon leaving just enough to tuck in at the top. Secure the tucked-in ribbon end with fabric glue.

EMMA LYTH aka BEAUBUTTONS

Emma spends her days feeding her button obsession by meticulously sourcing beautiful, quirky, and unusual buttons to use in her renowned bouquet creations. An industry expert in alternative bridal bouquets with a natural eye for design and composition, Emma is inspired by the fabulous 1950s with a penchant for all things kitsch. See more of her designs online at www.beaubuttons.co.uk

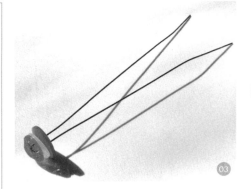

TIP

One large spool of floral tape should be sufficient for a small bouquet. It neatens the wired stems and helps keep the bouquet's shape.

BLACKBOARD FEATHER
NAPKIN RINGS

DECORATE YOUR PLACE SETTINGS WITH THESE SIMPLE BUT ELEGANT NAPKIN RINGS.
THE COLORS CAN BE MATCHED TO YOUR WEDDING THEME, AND THE CARDBOARD
FEATHERS ARE COVERED WITH BLACKBOARD PAINT SO THEY CAN BE USED AS PLACE
CARDS. INVITE YOUR GUESTS TO TAKE THEM HOME AS A REMINDER OF THE DAY.

TABLE PLACE-MARKER

HOW TO MAKE ... NAPKIN RINGS

SEE PAGE 90 FOR TEMPLATE

MATERIALS

COTTON FABRIC: ABOUT 2⅜" x 8" (6 x 20.5 cm) PER NAPKIN RING

PATTERNED SCRAPBOOKING PAPER

CARD STOCK: FLEXIBLE FOR THE NAPKIN RING AND STIFF FOR THE FEATHER

THIN COLORED CARD STOCK FOR THE NAPKIN RING BACKING

METALLIC EMBROIDERY THREAD

EYELETS AND EYELET SETTER

BLACKBOARD PAINT AND SMALL PAINTBRUSH

PENCIL AND RULER

CUTTING MAT, CRAFT KNIFE, AND SCISSORS

GLUE STICK AND HOLE PUNCH

CHALK OR CHALK MARKER

TIP

Cardboard cereal boxes are also a perfect recycled material for creating the rings, and board-backed envelopes are great for creating the feathers.

01 Cut a strip of flexible card stock measuring 1⅜" x 6¾" (3.5 x 17 cm), then cut a piece of your cotton fabric approx ⅜" (1 cm) larger all the way around. Cover one side of the card with glue and place it sticky-side down onto the wrong side of the fabric, positioning it centrally. Spread more glue over the other side of the card, and then fold the fabric corners over diagonally, pressing down firmly onto the adhesive.

02 Fold the fabric over each of the four edges, again pressing down firmly onto the card strip. Choose a thin colored card to coordinate with your napkin fabric and cut a strip from it measuring approx 1⅛" x 6¼" (3 x 16 cm). Glue the strip of colored card to the back of the fabric-covered card to hide the raw edges of the fabric.

03 Curve the ends of the covered strip around so that they overlap by ⅜" (1 cm), and punch a hole through both ends where they overlap. Feed an eyelet through the holes, and squeeze it shut with the eyelet setter, to hold the ring in place (alternatively, use a paper fastener).

04 Trace the feather template onto patterned paper and cut out. Trace a second feather onto thick card and carefully cut out using a craft knife, working on a cutting mat to protect your work surface.

05 Paint the cardboard feather with one or two coats of blackboard paint, and set aside to dry. For an extra-neat finish, you can also paint the back of the cardboard feather, choosing a color to coordinate with the fabric.

06 Cut a length of metallic thread measuring approx 12" (30.5 cm) long. Hold the two feathers together over the front of the ring (patterned paper and blackboard sides facing up) and tie in place with the thread. Finally, use a chalk marker to add the name of your guest to the blackboard feather.

01

02

KIRSTY NEALE

Kirsty is a freelance writer and designer. She specializes in fabric and paper and enjoys combining new materials with vintage or repurposed finds. Her work has been published in numerous books and magazines, and she blogs at www.kirstyneale.typepad.com

03

04

05

06

LANTERN WRAPS

USE GLASS PAINT AND SIMPLE STITCHED BANDS OF FELT TO TRANSFORM GLASS JARS INTO COLORFUL LANTERNS. A GROUP OF THREE MAKES A WONDERFUL WAY TO LIGHT UP THE CENTER OF EACH GUEST TABLE AT A WEDDING RECEPTION. FOR SAFETY'S SAKE, THESE LANTERNS SHOULD ONLY BE USED WITH BATTERY-OPERATED TEA-LIGHTS.

DRESS UP YOUR GLASS JARS

HOW TO MAKE ... LANTERN WRAPS

MATERIALS

THREE CLEAN GLASS JARS PER GUEST TABLE

FELT: RED, ORANGE, AND TURQUOISE

EMBROIDERY FLOSS: RED, ORANGE, AND TURQUOISE

PEBEO VITREA 160 GLASS PAINT: PEPPER RED, PAPRIKA, AND TURQUOISE

ASSORTED GLASS BEADS IN RED, ORANGE, AND TURQUOISE

CRAFT WIRE, 20 GAUGE

SCISSORS, THIN CARD, PENCIL, AND PAPER

TAPE MEASURE, BALLPOINT PEN, AND TRANSPARENT RULER

EMBROIDERY SCISSORS, EMBROIDERY NEEDLE, PAPER CLIPS, AND PINS

SMOOTH MAKEUP SPONGES AND PAINT TRAY

BAKING TRAY AND FOIL

PAIR OF PLIERS AND WIRE CUTTERS

01 Trace off the butterfly and heart templates and transfer onto thin card. Make a wrap template from paper, measuring it to the jar circumference plus a ¾" (2 cm) overlap. Use the wrap template to cut out three felt rectangles, one from each color.

02 Use the heart and butterfly templates and a ballpoint pen to mark out the cutwork design onto the felt rectangles starting in the middle, using a transparent ruler to keep the design level. Use embroidery scissors to make a small V-shaped cut in the middle of each shape, and cut outward to carefully follow the marked outlines.

03 Use three strands of contrasting thread to sew a line of running stitch around the large heart and along the top and bottom edges.

04 Wrap the felt around the jar and use paper clips to hold the ends together. Carefully slide the wrap off, pin, then secure with a line of running stitches.

05 To paint the jars, place one hand inside the jar and apply the paint with your other hand. Dab the

makeup sponge in the glass paint, wiping off the excess onto the edge of the paint tray. Apply the paint in smooth, fast strokes, covering the base first, then painting the sides, spreading it thinly for a tinted effect. Use long vertical strokes starting just under the rim and finishing at the base, leaving the rims unpainted. Leave the jars to dry upside down for a minimum of 24 hours.

LAURA HOWARD aka LUPIN

Laura is a not-quite grown-up girl who likes to make and do and is completely obsessed with felt. She shares free tutorials and writes about her crafty adventures on her blog bugsandfishes.blogspot.com and sells her work at www.lupin.bigcartel.com

SEE PAGE 90 FOR TEMPLATES

06 Put the jars right side up on a foil-covered baking tray, place in an oven set to 325°F (160°C), and bake for 40 minutes. Leave to cool completely before removing.

07 Make a wire handle to fit each jar. Cut one piece of wire to sit just under the rim, wrapping it around twice, allowing 1"–2" (2.5–5 cm) extra at each end. Cut a second piece of wire for the handle itself, making an upside-down U-shape, again allowing a little extra.

08 Bend one end of the handle upward. Thread on some glass beads at the other end, then bend upward too. Hook the beaded handle onto the wire circle; carefully place the circle under the rim. Pull the circle tight, and twist the ends together to secure.

09 Adjust the position of the handle, then wrap the ends around it to hold it in place. Trim excess wire and bend the wire ends neatly in place. Slip the felt wraps onto the jars.

EXPRESS YOURSELF
PLACE SETTING

UNLEASH YOUR GUESTS' CREATIVITY AT YOUR WEDDING RECEPTION. MAKE EACH PLACE SETTING A FRAMED SPACE IN WHICH THEY CAN RECORD THEIR THOUGHTS OF YOUR SPECIAL DAY IN WORDS AND PICTURES, FROM HEARTFELT MESSAGES TO CARTOON SKETCHES. COVER CANS WITH PRETTY PATTERNED PAPERS, FILL WITH PENCILS, AND LEAVE IN THE CENTER OF EACH TABLE.

HOW TO MAKE ... PLACE SETTING

SEE PAGE 90 FOR TEMPLATES

MATERIALS

ONE ROLL OF PATTERNED WALLPAPER

ONE ROLL OF THICK LINING PAPER

SELECTION OF PATTERNED PAPERS TO COVER CANS AND PENCILS

CANS AND PENCILS FOR COVERING

CLIP PHOTO STANDS

TRACING PAPER AND PENCILS (HB AND 2H)

CUTTING MAT, CRAFT KNIFE, AND METAL RULER

NUMBER RUBBER STAMPS AND INK PAD

SCISSORS AND GLUE

TIP

Pretty wallpaper samples are perfect for making the frames, and small scraps of craft or wrapping paper are ideal for covering the cans and pencils. Smooth round pencils are easiest to cover.

01 To make the frame, cut a rectangle from the patterned paper measuring 15" x 12½" (38 x 31.5 cm). Fold it in half with right sides facing, then fold in half again. Use a soft HB pencil to trace the large frame template. Turn the tracing paper over and place the two straight edges on the folded edges of the paper. Use the harder 2H pencil to go over the tracing.

02 Cut out the shape using scissors around the shaped sections, and the metal ruler and craft knife for the straight lines. Open out the frame. Iron out the crease line to make the paper completely flat if you wish.

03 Cut out a rectangle from the lining paper measuring 6¾" x 11½" (17 x 29 cm). Glue around the inside edge of the lining paper rectangle, place the cut-out frame over the lining paper, and press down all around the edge to secure.

04 To make the small frame for the guest table number, follow steps 1 and 2, using the small frame template. Apply glue to the back of the patterned paper frame and stick it down onto a piece of lining paper cut larger than the frame. Use scissors to cut out around the shape

of the frame. Working in this way makes the frame a little stronger, and this will prevent it from bending when you put it in the clip photo stand. Use the number stamps to print the guest table number in the middle of the frame.

05 Cut out a piece of paper to cover the can: this should be a rectangle that is the same height as the can, which can be wrapped around the can with an overlap of approx ¾" (2cm). Apply glue to the inside edge of the overlap. Wrap the paper around the can and press the glued edge down firmly.

06 Cut out a piece of paper to cover a pencil: this should be a rectangle that is the same length as the pencil up to the start of the pointed end, which can be wrapped around the pencil with an overlap of about ⅜" (1 cm). Apply glue to the inside edge of the overlap, wrap the paper tightly around the pencil, and press the glued edge down firmly.

DESIGNED
BY CLARE
YOUNGS

TIP

Don't forget to delegate
the job of collecting up
the mats at the end of
the day.

CROSS-STITCH
WEDDING SAMPLER

COMMEMORATE THE BIG DAY WITH THIS STYLISH MODERN TAKE ON THE TRADITIONAL SAMPLER. FITTING INTO A STANDARD PHOTO FRAME, THE DESIGN CAN BE PERSONALIZED TO MAKE A FUTURE HEIRLOOM THAT WILL BE TREASURED FOR YEARS TO COME. THIS PROJECT IS PERFECT FOR BEGINNERS WITH AN ITCH TO STITCH.

FUTURE
HEIRLOOM

HUGO
+
CAMILLE
6.5.2015

HOW TO MAKE ... WEDDING SAMPLER

MATERIALS

ONE PIECE OF 32-COUNT MOCHA LINEN OR
EVENWEAVE FABRIC (OR 16-COUNT AIDA)
MEASURING 8" x 8" (20.5 x 20.5 CM)

EMBROIDERY FLOSS:
CREAM x 4⅓ YARDS (4 METERS) (ANCHOR
926/DMC 712); PALE PEACH x 2⅕ YARDS
(2 METERS) (ANCHOR 366/DMC 739)

STANDARD PHOTO FRAME 5" x 7"
(12.5 x 18 CM) (GLASS OPTIONAL)

MOUNT BACKING BOARD AND MASKING TAPE

USE OF PHOTOCOPIER, PAPER, SCISSORS,
AND GLUE FOR PERSONALIZING PATTERN

TAPESTRY NEEDLE SIZE 24 OR 26

MINI NO-SEW ROLLER FRAME 9" x 6"
(23 x 15 CM) OR EMBROIDERY HOOP
ABOUT 8" (20.5 CM) (OPTIONAL)

SMALL PAIR OF EMBROIDERY SCISSORS

CUTTING MAT, CRAFT KNIFE, AND METAL RULER

IRON AND TOWEL

01 Photocopy (or scan and print) the wedding sampler chart and the alphabet chart. Cut out the letters and numbers you need, arrange them in the shaded areas on the chart, and glue in place, taking care to match up the grid squares.

02 Take your fabric and find its center by folding it in half horizontally and then vertically. These fold lines correspond to the arrows marked at the side of the charted designs (indicating the chart center) and will ensure that you work your design centrally on the fabric. Mark the center point with a pin or needle, and place the fabric in the embroidery frame or hoop.

03 Cut a length of embroidery thread, separate a single strand, fold it in half, and thread the ends through the tapestry needle. When making your first half stitch, leave a couple of inches (a few centimeters) of thread at the back of the fabric (the end with the loop), then pass the needle and thread through the loop and pull closed to secure the thread without a knot.

TIP

You can choose your fabric and thread colors to match the couple's wedding theme. If you need extra room for a long name, choose a larger frame and amend the placement of the border as necessary.

SOPHIE SIMPSON
aka WHAT DELILAH DID

Sophie is the designer, writer, and compulsive stitcher behind embroidery business, What Delilah Did. A perpetual dreamer and period-drama obsessive, she most ardently wishes she'd been born centuries ago. Her first book *Storyland Cross Stitch* has recently been published.
www.whatdelilahdid.com

SEE PAGE 94 FOR CHARTS

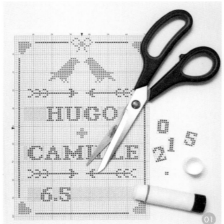

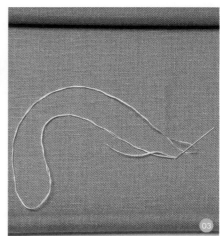

04 Working in sections from the center upward, stitch your personalized pattern. Each cross is stitched over two threads on linen or evenweave (see Charts, page 94, for instructions for working cross stitches). If working on 16-count aida, make each stitch over one block.

05 When the top half is complete, turn the frame upside down and stitch the rest of the pattern in sections from the center as before.

06 Remove the fabric from the frame and hand wash if necessary. Iron the embroidery face down over a towel to protect the stitches.

07 Measure and cut a piece of mount backing board just slightly smaller than your photo frame. Neatly stretch and fold the fabric around the board, tape into place, and insert into the frame.

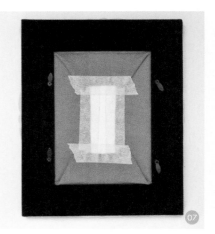

FLOWER INSPIRATIONS

01

Autumn Davidson of Autumn & Grace Bridal is a fabric florist specializing in repurposing vintage materials into memorable and personal heirloom bouquets. This tea-stained fabric bouquet (photographed by Aaron Wilcox) features vintage-garden hues, touches of satin greenery, and lace. To see more of her work, visit www.autumnandgracebridal.com

02

This stunning bouquet by Noaki Schwartz (photographed by Yuna Leonard) features a mix of red rhinestone jewelry set in gold and millinery roses against a bed of ivory cloth flowers. Pearls and faceted glass beads have been wired into the arrangement for added texture, and rhinestones set on the petals of the cloth flowers for a bit more sparkle. www.noakijewelry.com

03

Debbie Carlisle uses vintage buttons, jewelry, beads, and fabrics to create luxurious bespoke bridal bouquets for brides to treasure forever. Her hand-crafted heirloom designs come in every color of the rainbow. This small purple button posy works beautifully with a slim-line or tea-length prom-style wedding gown. www.dcbouquets.co.uk

BLOOMING LOVELY

04

Lindy Blake Miller of Atlanta, Georgia, makes exquisite vintage-book bouquets and corsages. The idea first came to her when she found a 100-year-old book destined for destruction and thought it would make a perfect "something old" for a bride's "something new," and so she began harvesting printed history for exceptional brides-to-be.
www.theepapergirl.etsy.com

05

A vintage jewelry corsage or buttonhole makes a lovely alternative to flowers and doubles as a gift to keep as a lasting reminder of your big day. Debbie Carlisle uses tiny vintage buttons, beads, and crystals to create her buttonholes, and each design is unique. www.dcbouquets.co.uk

06

Natural earthy hues are a great choice for the groomsmen's boutonnieres. Designed by Donni of Fairyfolk Weddings, the spring boutonniere combines natural feathers with vintage paper roses, and is wrapped in natural twine with a country check bow to finish. For more of Donni's whimsical designs, visit www.fairyfolkweddings.etsy.com

FUN TO SEW
TRUE LOVE PILLOWS

THESE PERSONALIZED PILLOWS ARE A GREAT WAY TO SEAT BRIDE AND GROOM IN COMFORT AND STYLE. LEATHER HEART APPLIQUÉS, INSPIRED BY 1950S ROCKABILLY TATTOOS, ARE TEAMED UP WITH CUTE POLKA DOTS AND POM-POMS. FOR A NAUTICAL FEEL, USE STRIPED FABRIC AND A GOLD ANCHOR MOTIF INSTEAD.

SITTING
PRETTY

HOW TO MAKE ... TRUE LOVE PILLOWS

MATERIALS (PER PAIR)

LEATHER: ONE PIECE OF RED MEASURING 8" x 8" (20.5 x 20.5 CM), ONE PIECE OF WHITE MEASURING 8" x 6¼" (20.5 x 16 CM), AND ONE PIECE OF BLACK MEASURING 2⅜" x 8" (6 x 20.5 CM)

1⅛ YARDS (1 METER) OF POLKA-DOT FABRIC

3¼ YARDS (3 METERS) OF POM-POM TRIM

BLACK EMBROIDERY FLOSS

SEWING THREAD

TWO PILLOW PADS MEASURING 14" x 14" (35.5 x 35.5 CM)

FABRIC GLUE

LEATHER NEEDLE, PINS, AND SCISSORS

SEWING MACHINE AND IRON

TIP

Always use a leather needle when sewing leather. It has a triangular tip that helps the needle to glide easily through, making it much easier to sew with. A thimble may also help.

01 Using the templates provided and working on the suede side of the leather, cut out the heart shape from red leather, and the scroll and two scroll ends from white leather.

02 Cut out the letters for the bride's name from a long strip of black leather 1⅛" (3 cm) high. Draw the outline of your letters IN REVERSE on the suede side of the leather, so that they will read the right way round. You may find it helpful to write them onto tracing paper first, then flip the tracing over to copy the name onto the suede.

03 Glue the cut-out letters onto the leather side of the scroll. Using a leather needle and black embroidery thread, hand stitch the letters in place, making sure that the corners in particular are securely stitched.

04 Now glue the scroll onto the leather side of the heart. Arrange the scroll ends and glue in place on the underside of the heart. Hand stitch all of the pieces into place with neat, straight stitches.

05 From the polka-dot fabric, cut one piece measuring 14½" (37 cm) square, and two rectangles measuring

8" x 14½" (20.5 x 37 cm) and 10¼" x 14½" (26 x 37 cm). Attach the leather heart in the center of the fabric square using a little glue, and hand stitch in place.

06 Cut four 14½" (37 cm) lengths of pom-pom trim and pin around the edges of the fabric square, with the pom-poms facing inward. Machine stitch using a small zigzag stitch.

ZOE LARKINS

Zoe Larkins is the inspired designer behind accessories label Love From Hetty & Dave, and she can often be found busily stitching away in her shop/studio in Bournemouth, England.
For more about her work, visit www.lovefromhettyanddave.co.uk

SEE PAGE 91 FOR TEMPLATES

01

03

07 Use the polka-dot fabric rectangles to make an envelope-opening cushion back. Prepare each rectangle by folding one long edge under by ¼" (6 mm), then fold over again by ⅜" (1 cm); press, pin, and machine stitch to complete the hemming.

08 Lay the heart appliqué right side up on your work surface. Place the smaller hemmed rectangle on top, right side facing down with raw edges aligning at the top and sides. Now position the larger hemmed rectangle to align the raw edges at the bottom and sides, so that it overlaps the smaller hemmed rectangle. Pin in place. Machine stitch slowly around the edges to avoid catching the pom-poms under the needle, carefully pushing them in as you sew if necessary.

09 Carefully snip off the corners and turn right side out. Use the point of your scissors to gently push out the corners before inserting the cushion pad. Now make a second cushion for the groom.

04

06

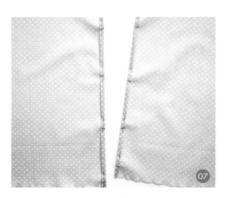

07

08

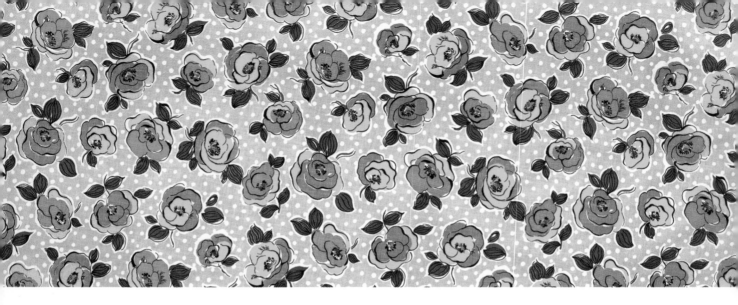

KOKESHI-STYLE
WEDDING DECORATION

MADE FROM EASY-TO-MOLD POLYMER CLAY, THIS TINY KOKESHI COUPLE CAN BE CUSTOMIZED TO RESEMBLE ANY BRIDE AND GROOM. MAKE THEM A FAUX-WOODEN DANCE FLOOR, COMPLETE WITH CONFETTI AND A STRING OF HEARTS, AND THEY'RE READY TO TAKE UP POSITION ON THE TOP TIER OF YOUR CAKE OR IN THE MIDDLE OF THE TOP TABLE.

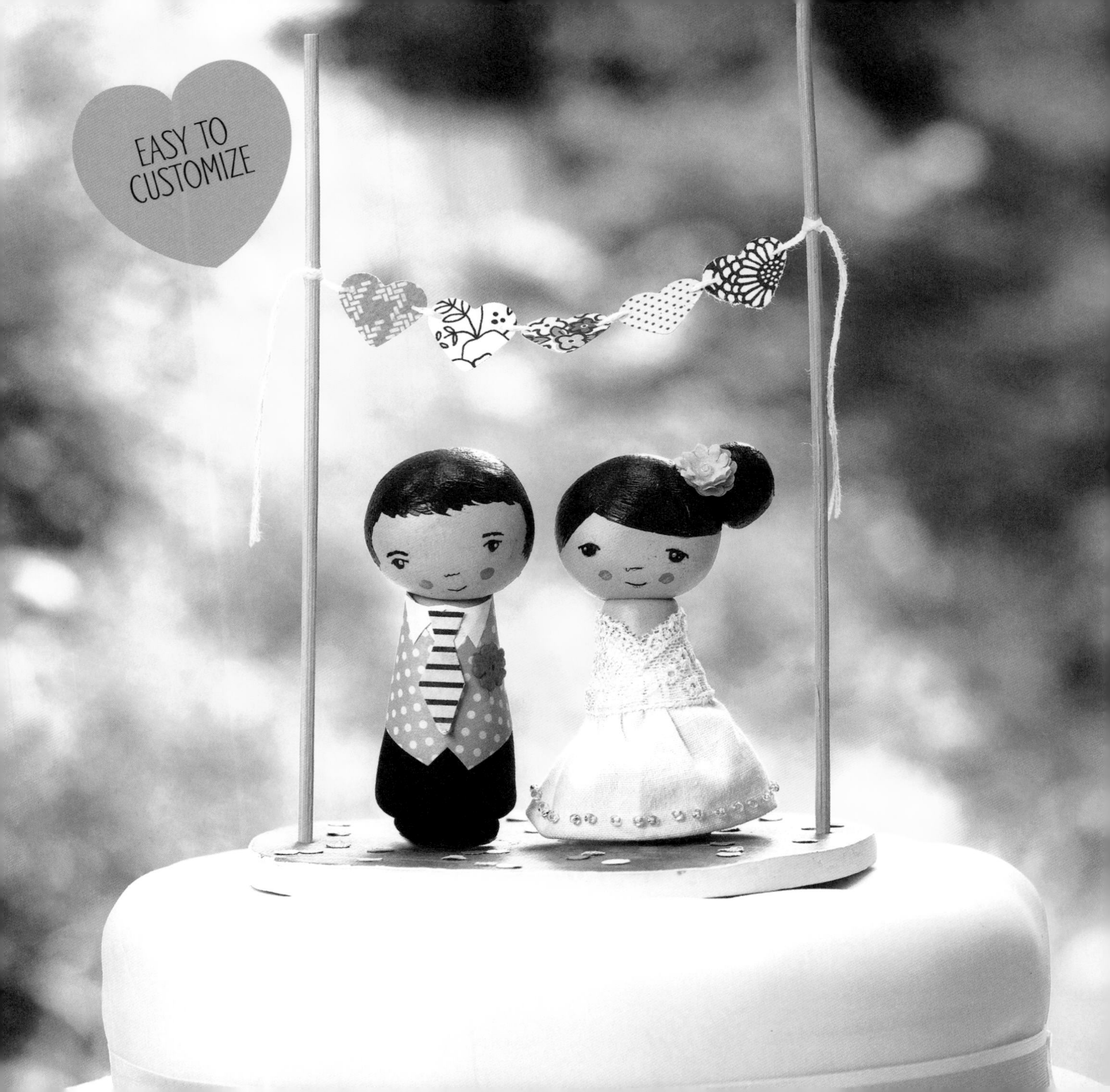
EASY TO
CUSTOMIZE

HOW TO MAKE ... WEDDING DECORATION

SEE PAGE 91 FOR TEMPLATES

MATERIALS

OVEN-BAKE MODELING POLYMER CLAY

ACRYLIC PAINT: BLACK, WHITE, PINK, AND SUITABLE COLORS FOR HAIR AND SKIN TONES

FINE BLACK MARKER PEN

SMALL SCRAPS OF PATTERNED AND WHITE PAPER

WOODGRAIN-PATTERNED PAPER

SMALL SCRAPS OF WHITE COTTON FABRIC AND SCALLOPED-EDGED LACE

SMALL EMBELLISHMENTS: PAPER OR FABRIC FLOWERS, AND SEED BEADS

TWO BAMBOO SKEWERS

KITCHEN SCALES, ROLLING PIN, AND BAKING SHEET

COTTON BUD, SMALL PAINTBRUSH, PENCIL, PVA GLUE, AND SCISSORS

ELASTIC BAND AND TOOTHPICKS

NEEDLE AND WHITE THREAD

HOLE PUNCH AND SMALL HEART PUNCH

01 For each figure, take three pieces of clay weighing just under an ounce (about 25g), just over an ounce (30g), and a small piece (5g). Roll the largest piece into a cone shape about 2" (5 cm) tall, and the other two into round balls. Flatten the smallest ball into a disk shape.

02 Press the disk onto the bottom of the cone. Gently push a toothpick partway down into the cone. Add the head on top, so the toothpick is completely hidden, and the head and body are securely joined together.

03 For the bride, roll another small ball of clay (about 5g) to make the bun for her hair. Break off a small piece of toothpick, and push one end into the ball. Push the other end into the side of the head. Bake the clay figures according to the manufacturer's instructions.

TIP
If the head and body become separated after baking, add a little PVA glue to the cocktail stick and the surface of the clay, press the join together firmly, and leave to dry before painting.

04 Paint the head and the neck and upper body of each figure using an appropriate flesh tone. Paint on the bride's dress and the groom's shirt in white, and use black for the groom's trousers.

05 Use a pencil to lightly draw on the facial features and hairline. Trace over the facial features with a fine black marker pen. Use the end of a toothpick to add a tiny dot of white paint to each eye, and a cotton bud to add dots of pink for the cheeks. Paint the hair using an appropriate color. For variations on hair and facial details see page 41.

06 To dress the groom, use the templates provided to cut a collar from white paper and a tie and waistcoat from patterned paper. Spread glue over the back of the waistcoat and wrap around the body, using an elastic band to hold it in place while the glue dries. Stick on the collar and tie, and add a small paper or fabric flower for the boutonniere.

HOW TO MAKE ... WEDDING DECORATION (CONTINUED)

DESIGNED BY KIRSTY NEALE

07 To dress the bride, cut a 1½" x 6" (3.8 x 15 cm) strip of white fabric. Fold over a narrow hem along the bottom edge and sew into place with running stitch, adding a single seed bead to each stitch. Sew a gathering stitch around the top edge of the skirt. Place the skirt around the bride's waist, pull the thread ends taut, then knot together.

08 Spread a thin layer of glue over the upper half of the bride's body and the top of her skirt. Cut a piece of scalloped-edged lace, lining it up in the center of the bride's torso for the sweetheart neckline. Press it down firmly and add a few stitches at the back to hold the ends securely together. Glue a paper flower to the bride's bun to finish.

09 To make the base, roll out a circle of clay about 5" (12.5 cm) in diameter and ¼" (6 mm) thick. Use a bamboo skewer to make a hole about ⅜" (1 cm) in from the edge at either side. Bake, and once the disk has completely cooled, cut out a circle of woodgrain-patterned paper and glue on top, re-marking the skewer holes.

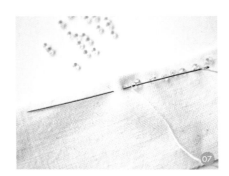

10 Hole punch through colored paper to make tiny pieces of confetti. Place the bride and groom figures in the center of the base, then sprinkle confetti randomly around them. Lift the figures away, and glue the confetti into place.

11 To make the banner, punch out five or six heart shapes from patterned paper. Cut a 20" (51 cm) length of white embroidery thread, and use a needle to thread it through the top edges of each heart.

12 Snip the pointed ends off two bamboo sticks, so that each measures about 6¾" (17 cm) tall. Push the skewers into the holes in the base. Tie on the heart banner adding a little glue over the knots, then trim the thread ends to the desired length. Finally, glue the bride and groom to the base, positioning them so that they are facing slightly toward each other.

HOW TO MAKE ... VARIATIONS

Give the groom a beard.

Add details to match
your bridal accessories.

Add a wavy or scalloped edge
to suggest curly hair.

Use a length of fancy braid or trim
to make a headdress.

Add extra balls of clay
to make a piled-high hairstyle.

Make a tiara from crystal
and pearl beads.

To make a pair of glasses, cut two 6¾" (17 cm) lengths of jewelry wire. Twist them together in the center, then use pliers to bend the pieces on either side into rectangles (right). Twist the wires together again at the outer edge of each rectangle, and snip off any excess. Bend the twisted ends so that they are at right angles to the frames to make arms (far right). Add a small amount of glue to the back of each arm and the twisted center section before pressing the glasses into place on the head.

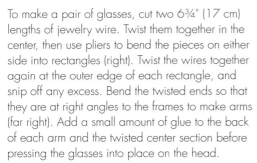

FOLDED FABRIC
CORSAGES & BOUTONNIERES

A WEDDING WOULDN'T BE A WEDDING WITHOUT AN ARRAY OF BEAUTIFUL BLOOMS. NOW YOU CAN BECOME YOUR OWN FABRIC FLORIST BY MAKING THESE BEAUTIFUL VINTAGE-STYLE CORSAGES AND BOUTONNIERES FOR ALL YOUR GUESTS. GORGEOUS ON THE DAY, THEY MAKE A LASTING SOUVENIR TO TAKE HOME.

VINTAGE STYLE

HOW TO MAKE ... CORSAGES & BOUTONNIERES

SEE PAGE 91 FOR TEMPLATES

MATERIALS

TONING SMALL-PRINT FABRICS OF YOUR CHOICE

SEWING THREADS TO MATCH

DOUBLE-SIDED FUSIBLE WEBBING

STIFF WIRE FOR FLOWER STEMS AND DECORATIVE CRAFT WIRE FOR LEAF STEMS

RIBBON

SEWING NEEDLE

PINKING SHEARS, DRESSMAKER'S SCISSORS, AND SCISSORS FOR CUTTING WIRE

SAFETY PINS AND FANCY-HEADED PINS

TIP

To make the flower for each corsage or boutonniere, you will need two toning small-print fabrics each measuring approx 14" x 14" (35.5 x 35.5 cm), as well as a little green fabric for the leaves. Cutting on the bias gives the petal shapes a little bit of stretch for a lovely curvy look.

01 Start by making a corsage. Fuse your chosen fabrics together with fusible webbing. Use the petal templates to cut seven small petals and eight large petals on the bias by placing templates diagonally on the fabric. Cut a ¾" x 12" (2 x 30.5 cm) fabric strip also on the bias.

02 Snip into the center of each petal. Gently fray the edges by using a pin to pull some of the threads free. Screw up into a tight ball and roll between your fingers. Open out, hold the corners, and tug. Repeat along one long edge of the fabric strip.

03 To make the flower center, roll one end of the fabric strip to give you a tight start, then work outward, coiling and twisting the fabric as you go. Tuck the loose end underneath and secure with a few stitches.

04 Add the smaller petals first. Overlap the slit fabric at the petal base for a curved shape and stitch to the back of the flower center. Add the next petal slightly overlapping the first, repeating to add all the small petals.

05 Attach the outer row of eight large petals as step 4. Use pinking shears to cut two large leaves from green fabric; fold in half and press the "vein" lines. Snip into the center at the base, overlap, and attach to the flower back. Sew a fabric circle over the back to fix a safety pin to.

JENNY DIXON

A craft journalist by trade, Jenny has always loved to make things. She is based in Bath in the UK, where she shares her home with an outrageously large fabric stash. Find her online at:
www.jennysbuttonjar.wordpress.com

06 To make a boutonniere, fuse fabrics together and cut out five large petals and a 1½" x 12" (3.8 x 30.5 cm) fabric strip, all on the bias. Gather the fabric strip to make the flower center: work small running stitches along one edge and pull tight. Start by rolling the strip tightly, then a little more loosely, until you reach the end; stitch through the base of the coil to secure.

07 Add each of the large petals in turn around the flower center: keep them close and upright, overlapping as you go. To give a more realistic look, roll the top edge of the petals and crease with your fingernail to hold in place. Cut a piece of wire for the stem and push it into the base. Use pinkng shears to cut a 1½" (3.8 cm) fabric circle and make a snip to the center. Fit the fabric circle around the stem and fold into a cone shape to fit neatly around the base of the flower, then stitch it in place.

08 Use pinking shears to cut three small leaves from bonded fabrics. Take a length of decorative craft wire, double it, twist it, and stitch it to the front of one of the leaves to create a central vein and stem. Repeat for the other two leaves, then twist the stems of all the leaves together to create the spray. Place the spray behind the flower and bind all the stems together tightly with ribbon, stitching the end to fasten. Use fancy-headed pins to attach the boutonnieres.

CUT AND PRINT

WEDDING INVITES

USE SIMPLE PAPER CUTTING AND LINO-PRINTING TECHNIQUES TO CREATE PERSONALIZED, HAND-CRAFTED WEDDING INVITATIONS INSPIRED BY POLISH PAPER FOLK ART DESIGNS. THERE ARE TWO DESIGNS FOR YOU TO CHOOSE FROM, AND EACH CAN BE EASILY CUSTOMIZED WITH YOUR OWN INITIALS.

HANDMADE
INVITATIONS

HOW TO MAKE ... WEDDING INVITES

MATERIALS

PIECES OF WHITE CARD STOCK
MEASURING 6" x 12" (15 x 30.5 CM)

PIECES OF COLORED PAPER
MEASURING 6" x 6" (15 x 15 CM)

SPEEDY CARVE LINO BLOCK
AND LINO CUTTER

INK PADS IN COLORS OF YOUR CHOOSING

LINO ROLLER OR BRAYER

MINIATURE HEART PUNCH

TRACING PAPER, PENCIL, AND ERASER

CUTTING MAT, CRAFT KNIFE, AND
METAL RULER

TIP

To make it easier to grip your stamp when printing, you can mount it onto a wood block using very strong glue.

01 To make the heart wreath invite, fold a piece of white card stock in half. Make a tracing of the heart wreath template, filling in all the leaves as solid shapes. Transfer the design onto the front of the folded card with the fold at the top.

02 Open the card out flat on the cutting mat. Use a craft knife to carefully cut away all of the areas of the heart design shaded in pencil, making sure to leave gaps in the design as marked on the template: These strengthen the card to prevent it from flopping over when standing. Erase any remaining pencil marks, and glue a square of colored paper to the inside back of the card.

03 Make a lino-cut stamp of the bride and groom's initials. Transfer your design onto a small rectangle of speedy carve lino block, using your fingernail to rub the traced image on. Your letters should appear reversed and mirrored so that they will print the right way around.

04 Use the lino cutter to carefully cut away all the areas that you do not want to print, leaving the pencil lines uncut to form your stamp.

05 Make a test print: press the ink pad firmly over the stamp, and use a lino roller or brayer over the back of the stamp to achieve an even print. Make any adjustments to your stamp before using it to print the initials in the center of the paper-cut heart.

SEE PAGE 91 FOR TEMPLATES

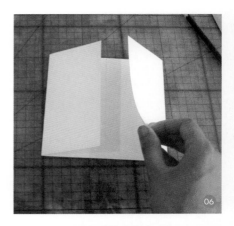

06 To make the bird invite, take a piece of white card stock, mark the midway point on each long side, and fold the edges into the center to give you a gatefold card.

07 Use the bird template to trace the bird design (one in reverse) onto two small squares of lino block. Personalize the bird stamps with the bride and groom's initials, remembering to reverse letters as necessary so they read correctly when printed. Use the lino cutter to cut away all the areas that you don't want to print and trim away any excess from the outer edge of the design.

08 Make a test print before using the finished stamps to print the birds facing each other, one on each side of the front of the gatefold card.

09 Open the card out flat and punch out a heart border along the top and bottom edges of the gatefold. Refold and glue a colored paper square to the center panel of the inside of the card.

ZEENA SHAH

Zeena Shah studied printed textile design at Chelsea School of Art & Design and has since worked in both the fashion and interiors textile industry before launching her own label, z e e n a—a collection of hand silk screen printed and handmade textiles for the home.
www.zeenashah.com

FELT APPLIQUÉ
RING PILLOW

INSPIRED BY BRIGHT FLORAL PRINTS OF THE 1960'S AND 1970'S, THIS SMALL
PILLOW, DECORATED WITH A PROFUSION OF COLORFUL FELT FLOWERS AND SPARKLY
SEED BEADS, IS PERFECT FOR KEEPING YOUR WEDDING RINGS SAFE ON YOUR BIG DAY.
IT HAS A USEFUL CARRYING STRAP ON THE BACK FOR LITTLE HANDS.

HOW TO MAKE ... RING PILLOW

SEE PAGE 92 FOR TEMPLATES

MATERIALS

ONE PIECE OF IVORY FELT
MEASURING 10¼" x 14½" (26 x 37 CM)

ONE PIECE EACH OF ORANGE,
YELLOW-ORANGE, YELLOW, CORAL, CANDY
PINK, AND PALE PINK FELT MEASURING
ABOUT 4¼" x 6¾" (11 x 17 CM)

ONE PIECE OF PEACH FELT
MEASURING ABOUT 3½" x 5½" (9 x 14 CM)

ONE PIECE OF BRIGHT PINK FELT
MEASURING APPROX 5½" x 6¼" (14 x 16 CM)

SEWING THREADS TO MATCH FELT COLORS

EMBROIDERY FLOSS: CORAL, ORANGE,
YELLOW, PALE PINK, AND BRIGHT PINK

SEED BEADS IN MATCHING COLORS
(SIZE 8/0)

NARROW LIGHT PINK RIBBON, ABOUT 10¼"
(26 CM)

POLYESTER STUFFING

SCISSORS, EMBROIDERY SCISSORS,
NEEDLES, AND PINS

01 Use the templates provided to cut out all the flower pieces marked A–E in the quantities and colors marked on the templates. From the ivory felt, cut out two 7" (18 cm) squares for the pillow front and back, and a rectangle measuring 2½" x 5" (6.5 x 12.5 cm) for the carry strap.

02 Take one of the ivory felt squares and place pieces 1 and 2 of flowers A–D as shown in the photo, with the flowers slightly overhanging at the edges. Using double-thickness ivory sewing thread, sew a small cross stitch in the center of each flower.

03 Using three strands of the embroidery thread (coral for flower A, yellow for B, bright pink for C, and orange for D), sew lines of running stitch radiating from the center of each flower.

04 Sew pieces 1 and 2 of flower E in the pillow center, adding lines of pale pink running stitch as in the photo. Now add pieces A3, B3, C3, and D3, sewing on with matching sewing thread.

05 Cut out small flowers and circles in assorted colors to fill in the gaps between the large flowers.

06 Add the remaining pieces E3 and E4 to the central flower, and sew a line of running stitch around the center circle with matching sewing thread.

07 To embellish the corner flowers, sew clusters of seed beads, starting in the middle and working outward in circles. Sew each bead in position with a double thickness of sewing thread to match the bead color. Add a single seed bead to the infill flowers and circles. Sew the midpoint of the ribbon to the center of the pillow, having trimmed the ribbon ends at an angle to help prevent fraying.

TIP

For the precise cutting of the felt flowers, use embroidery scissors. It may also help to use transparent parcel tape rather than pins to fix the paper templates to the felt.

02

03

04

08 To make the carrying strap, pin the felt rectangle in the center of the undecorated ivory square and stitch one or two lines of backstitch along each of the short ends. Remove pins.

09 Place the pillow front and back together with right sides facing out, and pin. The top (front) square may have shrunk slightly from the appliqué stitching, so if necessary trim any excess felt from the bottom (back) square so that back and front match exactly. Blanket stitch together, folding the flower petals out of the way as you sew past them, and leaving a small gap for stuffing.

10 Stuff the pillow gradually with small pieces of stuffing for an even finish, then blanket stitch the opening closed.

05

06

DESIGNED BY LAURA HOWARD

07

08

09

CARVED HEARTS
TABLE CENTERPIECE

THIS NATURE-THEMED TABLE SETTING MAKES GREAT USE OF NATURAL MATERIALS LIKE STACKED LOGS. THE TABLE NUMBER AND THE BRIDE AND GROOM'S INITIALS ARE "CARVED" INTO CARD HEARTS MADE FROM RECYCLED CARDBOARD. FAUX CHIC! REAL PINE CONES ARE USED AS PLACE HOLDERS TO GUIDE YOUR GUESTS TO THEIR SEATS.

WOODLAND WEDDING

HOW TO MAKE ... TABLE CENTERPIECE

MATERIALS

THICK CARDBOARD

TWO LOGS (ONE LARGE, ONE SMALLER) FOR EACH GUEST TABLE

PINE CONES, ONE FOR EACH GUEST

TWINE

GOOD-QUALITY WRITING PAPER

COLD COFFEE AND SOFT PAINTBRUSH

CUTTING MAT, CRAFT KNIFE, AND SCISSORS

PENCIL AND MARKER PEN

SCREWDRIVER

GAS LIGHTER

TIP
If you want a less rustic look, you could spray paint the pine cones to match your wedding color scheme.

01 To make the guest table number, cut a heart shape from thick cardboard. While you could use a heart template as a guide to the shape, you will get a more realistic result if you draw the shape freehand. Use a craft knife to cut out your heart shape.

02 Working on the cutting mat to protect your work surface, use the screwdriver to make two holes at the top of the heart. If you don't have a cutting mat, place a piece of poster-tack beneath the heart where you want to pierce the holes.

03 Use a pencil to write the guest table number in the middle of the heart. Use the craft knife to go over the number a couple of times, just enough to remove the top surface of the cardboard, to make an incision to give the impression that the number has been carved out.

04 Paint the cardboard heart with several coats of strong, cold coffee to color it brown (at least three or four). This will make your cardboard heart look more like a piece of wood. To avoid over-wetting the cardboard, be sure to allow a few minutes between coat applications. Leave to dry thoroughly.

05 Once the cardboard heart has dried completely, use the gas lighter to carefully singe its edges to give the impression of the tree bark. For safety's sake, it is a good idea to use a pair of fireproof gloves and to have a bowl of water on hand. Move the flame quickly over the front surface of the heart to distress the carved number further if you wish.

06 Cut a length of twine long enough to wrap around the smaller log and thread it through the holes pierced in the heart. Tie the heart in place.

07 Follow steps 1–6 to make a larger heart decorated with the bride and groom's initials, and tie this around the larger log.

08 Assemble the table centerpiece. Put the small log on top of the large log, positioning it slightly to one side. Place a few pine cones alongside the small log to finish.

09 To make the pine cone place cards, cut rectangles of paper measuring about 2⅜" x 1½" (6 x 3.8 cm) and write on the names of your guests. Now simply insert the tags in the pine cones, making sure that the names can be clearly seen.

01

02

03

04

05

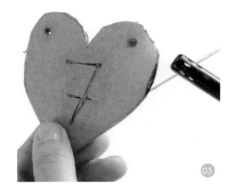

07

SEE PAGES 91 &
93 FOR HEART
TEMPLATES

ILARIA CHIARATTI

Italian-born Ilaria lives in the
Netherlands with her husband. She
works as a freelance photographer
for the Italian magazine *Casa Facile*
and her work has been published
in France, China, and Russia. She
also runs her own company, IDA
Interior LifeStyle, an interior design
consultancy. She shares her interior
styling inspirations and her crochet
work on her blog at
www.idainteriorlifestyle.com

WEDDING DAY DREAMS

SWEET CAKE TOPPERS

01

A cheese wedding cake is a tasty alternative to the traditional iced cake, and these adorable mice, with their heart-entwined tails, make the perfect decoration to sit on the very top layer. They are made from polymer clay by Melina and Marina Nazarians, twin sisters from southern California. To view more of their handmade collection, visit www.melimaristudio.etsy.com

02

Based in Ljubljana, the capital city of Slovenia, Mojca of CherryTime makes all sorts of lovely things from crochet, including unique and personalized cake toppers. From koi to clown fish, or fish in any color of the rainbow, she prides herself on being able to customize each happy pair. www.cherrytime.etsy.com

03

Melanie Ann Green's needle-felted snowy owls make the perfect cake topper for a winter wedding. They are made from natural white merino wool with sweet little silver wire legs. To see more of her amazing designs, visit Melanie's felt menagerie at www.feltmeupdesigns.co.uk

SPECIAL TOUCHES

04

Paper Polaroid is a husband-and-wife team making a crafty living in Lancaster County, Pennsylvania. Their decorative paper creations include these romantic paper hearts on sticks, which make wonderfully colorful wedding favors. www.PaperPolaroid.etsy.com

05

Meg, the collage artist behind Vintage Scraps, creates journals, art, and cards using forgotten bits of antique papers. These journals feature original vintage wedding dress pattern illustrations, antique buttons, and lace, and they make great retro-look wedding guest books. For more of Meg's designs, visit www.VintageScraps.etsy.com

06

These robin's nest place cards are a whimsical way to decorate guest tables at the reception, to guide family and friends to take their places. They were designed by Donni of Fairyfolk Weddings, who is brimming with ideas for natural woodland weddings at www.FairyfolkWeddings.etsy.com

MACHINE APPLIQUÉ
PHOTO ALBUM COVER

PHOTOGRAPHS CAPTURE MEMORIES OF THE DAY THAT THE NEW COUPLE CAN CHERISH FOREVER. A HANDMADE CUSTOMIZED ALBUM COVER, DECORATED IN THE STYLE AND COLORS OF YOUR WEDDING, BRINGS BACK THE EMOTIONS OF THE DAY AT FIRST GLANCE, WITHOUT YOU EVEN HAVING TO PEEK INSIDE!

MEMORIES TO SHARE

elsa ♡ thomas
5.4.2015

HOW TO MAKE ... PHOTO ALBUM COVER

SEE PAGE 92 FOR TEMPLATES

MATERIALS

PHOTOGRAPH ALBUM 9½" (24 CM) HIGH BY 8½" (21.5 CM) WIDE BY ¾" (2 CM) DEEP

COTTON/LINEN BLEND FABRIC: TWO PIECES FOR THE FRONT AND BACK COVER EACH MEASURING 10¼" x 8¼" (26 x 20.5 CM) AND TWO PIECES FOR THE INSIDE PANELS EACH MEASURING 10¼" x 5" (26 x 12.5 CM)

ONE PIECE OF FLORAL FABRIC FOR THE SPINE MEASURING 10¼" x 4" (26 x 10 CM)

ONE PIECE OF FLORAL FABRIC FOR THE LINING MEASURING 10¼" x 18½" (26 x 47 CM)

SCRAPS OF FLORAL FABRIC FOR THE APPLIQUÉ

DOUBLE-SIDED FUSIBLE WEBBING

RIBBON AND EMBROIDERY FLOSS IN COLORS TO MATCH THE FLORAL FABRICS

GOOD-QUALITY BLACK SEWING THREAD

EMBROIDERY HOOP AND DARNING/ EMBROIDERY MACHINE PRESSER FOOT

SEWING MACHINE, PENCIL, IRON, SCISSORS, PINS, AND NEEDLE

01 Pin the floral fabric spine on top of the cotton/linen front piece with right sides facing, lining up along the left edge. Machine stitch using a ⅜" (1 cm) seam allowance. Press the seams open.

02 Trace the birds, ribbon banner, and heart templates onto pieces of double-sided fusible webbing. Use an iron to press the motifs onto the back of your chosen fabric scraps, then cut out carefully around the marked outlines.

03 Peel off the paper backing from the fusible webbing, position the motifs on the album cover front and iron in place. Hoop up the fabric and attach the darning/embroidery foot to your sewing machine.

04 Drop the machine's feed dogs and, using the black thread, freehand

TIP
To calculate the fabric measurements to suit a different sized photo album, measure the width of your album, double it, add the depth of the spine, then add a ⅜" (1 cm) seam allowance all around the edge.

machine embroider around the shapes twice. Add the shading on the ribbon banner, the eyes to the birds, and the trailing ribbon to the hanging heart. Trim and neaten the threads at the front and back. Remove the hoop.

05 Now work the hand embroidery. Use a pencil to lightly mark the first names and wedding date onto the ribbon banner. Use a light box (or hold the fabric up against a window) to trace the flower embroidery pattern and corner motifs onto the fabric.

06 Use backstitch to embroider the names/date, and follow the stitch advice on the embroidery patterns for working the flower embroidery and the corner motifs in thread colors to match your fabrics. Complete the running stitch border around the edge of the cover.

07 With right sides facing, pin the cotton/linen back piece to the raw edge of the spine and machine stitch together with a ⅜" (1 cm) seam allowance. Press the seams open. Hem one long edge on each of the cotton/linen fabric inside panels. With the right side of the album

cover facing up, pin the inside panels in place, aligning the raw edges and sandwiching a piece of ribbon centrally at each side (for the ties). Machine stitch around the raw edges with a ¼" (6 mm) seam allowance.

08 Pin the lining fabric on top with right sides facing, and machine stitch around the edge of the cover using a ⅜" (1 cm) seam allowance, leaving a 1⅛" (3 cm) gap at the base of the spine for turning through. Snip the corners and turn the finished cover the right way out. Press and slip stitch the opening closed by hand.

EMILY CARLILL

Emily Carlill crafted her own DIY wedding in 2011. She continues to make lots more wedding crafts for others as well as running her crafty business Love Me Sew, designing and creating craft packs and holding sewing workshops. For more, see www.emilycarlill.com and www.lovemesew.co.uk

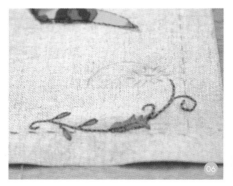

STITCHED FELT
GOOD LUCK CHARMS

IT IS A TRADITION TO GIVE THE BRIDE A TOKEN TO HOLD ON HER WEDDING DAY, TO WISH HER WELL AND BESTOW HER WITH GOOD LUCK. DIFFERENT CULTURES HAVE DIFFERENT GOOD LUCK SYMBOLS. FOR EXAMPLE, IN CHINA, A TURTLE REPRESENTS WEALTH, LONGEVITY, AND GOOD HEALTH; AND THERE ARE THREE MORE DESIGNS FOR YOU TO CHOOSE FROM.

TRADITIONAL
FUN

HOW TO MAKE ... GOOD LUCK CHARMS

MATERIALS

FELT: DARK GRAY, LIGHT GRAY, BABY PINK, CANDY PINK, WHITE, AND PISTACHIO GREEN

EMBROIDERY FLOSS OR SEWING THREADS IN SHADES TO MATCH FELT COLORS

SMALL AMOUNT OF POLYESTER STUFFING

⅜" (1 CM) WIDE SATIN RIBBON IN SHADES TO MATCH YOUR FELT COLORS

PINS, SHARP NEEDLE, AND SMALL, SHARP SCISSORS

TIP

Use a medium-density felt—you can change the colors of the charms to match your wedding color scheme. If you don't have any polyester stuffing, cotton balls will work just as well.

01 Start by cutting out two identical backing shapes for the base of each of the charms using the templates provided. The backing shape is the outer outline on each of the templates, and these should be cut from a contrasting felt color so that the appliqué really stands out: candy pink has been used for the cat, dark gray for the turtle, and white for the cake and horseshoe.

02 Using the templates and the finished project photograph on page 65 to guide you, cut out all the other pieces of felt that you will need to complete each charm appliqué. Use small sharp scissors to cut the intricate pieces as neatly as possible.

03 Now begin layering and stitching the small details onto the front pieces, such as the ears, eyes, and nose onto the cat's head, and the belly and heart onto the cat's body. Use thread to match the felt piece being sewn on, working small back stitches with a sharp embroidery needle. Sew on very small pieces, like the cat's pupils, with tiny cross stitches.

04 Once the front appliqué is layered and stitched, pin the pieces onto one of the backing shapes.

05 Start stitching around the edge of the appliquéd pieces to secure them in place, working your back stitches approx ¹⁄₁₆" (2mm) from the edge to mirror the outline of the design. Add any additional stitched details such as the small stitch beneath the cat's nose for the mouth and the progressively longer stitches at either side of the nose for the whiskers.

06 Once all the stitching on the front piece is complete, pin it to the remaining backing piece, taking care to line up front and back as neatly as possible. Blanket stitch around the edge of the charm, leaving a gap for stuffing at the top of the design. Gently fill the charm with stuffing (or cotton wool) but do not overstuff it, as the stuffing may become visible through the blanket stitch edge.

07 Make a small hanging loop from a short length of ribbon, slip it into the stuffing gap and stitch the opening closed. For the horseshoe charm, both of the top edges are left open for stuffing, and a longer length of ribbon is inserted into each opening to make a handle for carrying.

SEE PAGE 93 FOR TEMPLATES

01

02

CHARLIE MOORBY
aka THE SAVVY CRAFTER

Charlie is a thrifty craft blogger and incurable stitching addict with a penchant for anything handmade. Commissioning editor by day and crafter by night, you'll find her collecting buttons and hoarding ribbons on a daily basis. She's a dab hand with a pencil and loves a spot of cross stitching too. Find her online at www.thesavvycrafter.com

03

04

05

06

07

TIP

The turtle, the horseshoe, and the wedding cake charms are made in exactly the same way as the cat. The addition of extra lengths of ribbon on some of the charms adds an extra celebratory touch.

LACE EMBOSSED
WEDDING FAVORS

MANY COUPLES ENJOY GIVING WEDDING GUESTS A LITTLE GIFT. THESE PRETTY LITTLE BAGS ARE SIMPLE TO MAKE FROM BROWN PAPER AND CAN BE FILLED WITH ANY SWEET TREAT. SEAL EACH WITH A TAG EMBOSSED WITH THE NAMES OF THE HAPPY COUPLE AND TIE IN PLACE WITH SOME PRETTY VINTAGE LACE LAID OVER A MINIATURE DOILY.

FILL WITH
SWEET TREATS

HOW TO MAKE ... WEDDING FAVORS

SEE PAGE 93 FOR TEMPLATES

MATERIALS

WHITE AIR-DRY MODELING CLAY

THICK BROWN PAPER

LACE RIBBON

MINIATURE DOILIES

PATTERNED RUBBER STAMP AND MINIATURE ALPHABET STAMPS

SWEET TREATS

TRACING PAPER, THIN CARD STOCK, AND PENCILS (HB AND 2H)

ROLLING PIN AND NAIL FILE

CUTTING MAT, CRAFT KNIFE, METAL RULER

MASKING TAPE AND GLUE STICK

SINGLE HOLE PUNCH AND PAINTBRUSH

TIP

You can choose a patterned paper and any style of ribbon to fit in with the color scheme of your wedding.

01 Roll out some modeling clay to about ⅛" (3 mm) thick. Trace off the heart template onto thin card stock, cut it out and use as a template to cut out the heart tags from the clay. For the oblong tags, use the width of a metal ruler to cut strips, then cut the strips into 3½" (9 cm) sections.

02 Use a pretty patterned rubber stamp to emboss the bottom of the tags, and the handle of a paintbrush to make a hole approx ⅜" (1 cm) down from the top of the tags. Use miniature alphabet stamps to press out the names (or just the initials) of the bride and groom onto the tags. Allow the tags to dry, then use a nail file to smooth off any rough edges.

03 Use a soft HB pencil to trace off the bag template. Turn the tracing paper over, secure the corners to the reverse side of the brown paper with masking tape and go over the marked lines with a hard 2H pencil to give you a nice, sharp outline.

04 Working on a cutting mat, use a metal ruler and a craft knife to cut out the outer edge of the bag shape. Score along all the inner lines and fold them inward to start forming the bag shape.

05 Run the glue stick along the length of the side strip, overlap this onto the front panel of the bag, and press down firmly. Fold in one of the long bottom flaps and run the glue stick along the inside of the other three flaps. Fold in the two small side flaps, then fold the second long flap over the top. Put your fingers inside the bag and press the base against a flat surface, so that the base is securely fixed in place.

06 Squeeze the front and back panels together at the top of the bag to form a crease down the center of the side panels extending by approx 4" (10 cm).

07 Fill the bag with your treats, then take a miniature doily and fold it over the top of the bag to make a closure. Use the single hole punch to make a hole centrally, about 1" (2.5 cm) from the top edge of the bag. Take a 12" (30.5 cm) length of ribbon, thread on one of the tags, then thread the ribbon end through the punched hole. Tie the ribbon in a bow along the top edge of the bag.

DESIGNED BY CLARE YOUNGS

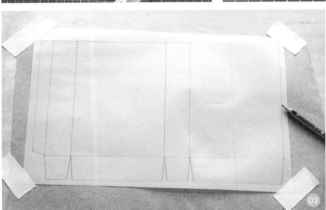

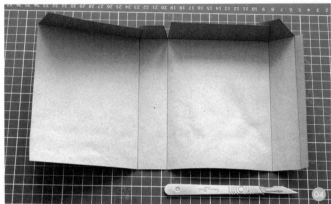

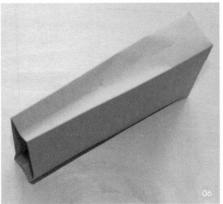

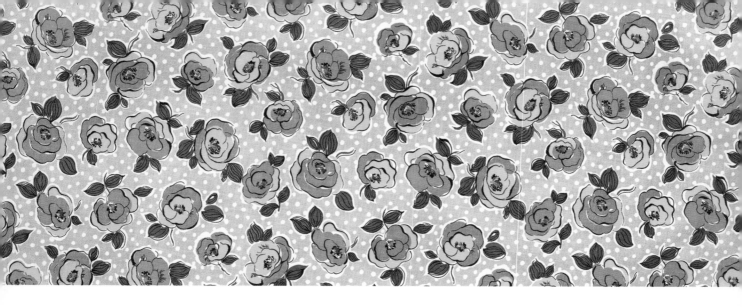

PAPER DECORATION
3D DIAMOND GARLAND

PRETTY PAPER 3D DIAMONDS CAN BE HUNG SINGLY AROUND YOUR WEDDING VENUE OR STRUNG TOGETHER TO MAKE BEAUTIFUL GARLANDS. MADE IN THREE DIFFERENT SIZES, EACH IS CUT AND FOLDED FROM WATERCOLOR PAPER, PAINTED, EMBELLISHED, AND FINISHED WITH A TASSEL.

INSPIRED BY PAPER LANTERNS

HOW TO MAKE ... 3D DIAMOND GARLAND

MATERIALS

WATERCOLOR PAPER (140LB/300GSM)

WATERCOLOR PAINTS

GOLD LEAF

PATTERNED PAPER

EMBROIDERY THREADS AND YARN

CORD OR STRING

MASKING TAPE OR WASHI TAPE

TRACING PAPER AND PENCIL

CRAFT KNIFE AND METAL RULER

SCISSORS AND PAINTBRUSH

NARROW DOUBLE-SIDED ADHESIVE TAPE

SPRAY ADHESIVE AND GLUE STICK

01 Transfer the 3D diamond garland template onto the watercolor paper and cut it out. Score firmly along the dotted lines, then fold.

02 Brush one or two coats of watercolor paint onto the front of your cut out paper shape (the side without the marked lines) and leave to dry thoroughly.

03 To add gold leaf, mask off one of the triangles by edging it with masking tape or preferably washi tape, as this peels off more easily and is less likely to damage the surface of the paper. Covering the rest of the shape with scrap paper, spray adhesive onto the masked-off triangle. Peel off the tape and press gold leaf on top of the triangle, brushing away any excess at the edges.

TIP
Always make sure you use spray adhesive in a well-ventilated area, and preferably outdoors.

04 To add patterned paper, cut out a triangle from your chosen paper and run a glue stick over the back of it. Position the paper triangle right side up over one of the triangular sections on the watercolor-paper shape and press down carefully.

05 Cut a length of thread measuring 32" (81.5 cm) and fold it in half. Place it in the middle of the paper shape. Add strips of double-sided tape to the flaps, then fold the shape up into a 3D diamond by sticking each flap underneath the edge labeled with the corresponding letter—flap A under side A, flap B under side B, and so on. Make sure the folded thread goes through the center of the diamond as you fold.

06 Cut 15–20 pieces of yarn and thread, each measuring approx 10" (25.5 cm) long. Bundle the threads together and lay them over the loose threads at the bottom of the 3D diamond, using the loose thread to tie a double knot around the center of the bundle.

DESIGNED BY KIRSTY NEALE

TIP
This project requires a card-weight watercolor paper that is fairly substantial but still easy to fold. Hot-pressed is smoother and flatter, so is good to embellish with.

07 Bring all of the thread ends together, then cut an extra piece of thread and tie it around the top of the bundle to form the tassel. Trim the ends for a neat finish.

08 Repeat steps 1–7 to make more 3D diamonds, varying the sizes and colors. Cut a length of cord or string as long as you want your finished garland to be. Slide it through the loop at the top of each 3D diamond in turn, making a single knot to hold each in place.

SEE PAGE
92 FOR
TEMPLATE

PAINTED GLASS
FLOWER DISPLAY

UPCYCLE A SELECTION OF GLASS JARS AND BOTTLES INTO A STUNNING CENTERPIECE TO GRACE THE TABLES AT YOUR WEDDING RECEPTION. STENCIL ON PATTERNS USING METALLIC PAINTS. USE THE DECORATED GLASSWARE AS VASES FOR FRESHLY PICKED FLOWERS OR FILL WITH SMALL BRANCHES DECORATED WITH PRETTY HANDMADE PAPER FLOWERS.

RECYCLED
GLASSWARE

HOW TO MAKE ... FLOWER DISPLAY

MATERIALS

GLASS JARS AND BOTTLES

COPPER SPRAY PAINT

MINERAL SPIRITS

PAPER DOILIES, ADHESIVE TAPE
IN VARYING WIDTHS, DOT STICKERS,
AND TWINE

PATTERNED PAPER

HEART DECORATIONS

TWIGS AND SMALL BRANCHES

SCISSORS, STAPLER, AND GLUE

TIP

For the most pleasing results, use both matt and shiny copper spray paint. To make the composition of your centerpiece more interesting, choose different shapes and sizes when selecting jars and bottles.

01 Carefully clean your glass jars and bottles with mineral spirits and allow to dry thoroughly.

02 Prepare the jars and bottles for painting. Use paper doilies, adhesive tape in varying widths, dot stickers, and twine to create a range of different stencil effects when applying your copper spray paint.

03 When applying the copper spray paint, it is safest to work outdoors; if this is not possible, do make sure that doors and windows are left open for a well-ventilated work space. Place the jars in shallow boxes, or protect your work surface with newspaper. Shake the can well and spray 8–12" (20.5–30.5 cm) away from the jars and bottles. Allow the paint to dry for 6–8 hours.

04 Once the jars and bottles are completely dry, peel off the stencils carefully to reveal the glass beneath.

05 If you prefer a perfect look, clean off any imperfections with a cotton bud dipped into a little mineral spirits. However, a few wayward paint drips can add a certain charm.

DESIGNED BY ILARIA CHIARATTI

06 To make the paper flowers, cut eight rectangles from your patterned paper each measuring 4" x 14" (10 x 35.5 cm). Concertina-fold the rectangles so that the folds measure ³⁄₈" (1 cm).

07 Staple in the middle of each of the concertina-folded paper rectangles. Gently open the ends at either side, and staple the ends together to complete each of the paper flowers.

08 Use glue to apply a heart decoration in the center of the flowers. To make a hanging loop, tie a small piece of twine around one of the stapled ends.

09 Place the painted jars and bottles in the center of the table, fill with small branches and twigs, and hang up the paper flowers.

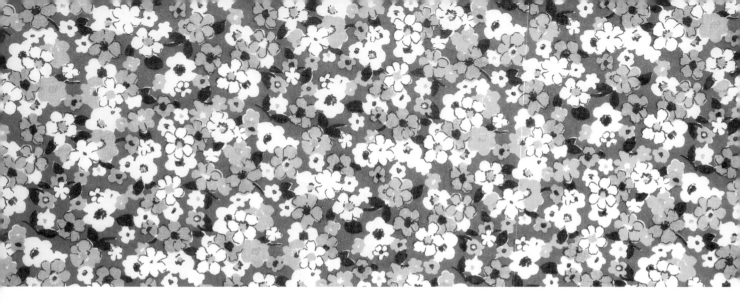

NEEDLE-FELT
CAKE TOPPER

THIS ADORABLE PAIR OF PLUMP POLAR BEARS MAKES THE CUTEST DECORATION FOR THE TOP OF YOUR WEDDING CAKE. THEY CAN BE CUSTOMIZED WITH YOUR OWN SPECIAL TOUCHES. YOU COULD, FOR EXAMPLE, MAKE A TOP HAT FOR THE GROOM OR A TIARA AND VEIL FOR THE BRIDE. YOU COULD ALSO PLACE FLOWER OR HEART-SHAPED BUTTONS BETWEEN THE PAWS.

DARLING DUO

HOW TO MAKE ... CAKE TOPPER

MATERIALS

50G OF WHITE OR CREAM MERINO ROVING
FOR EACH POLAR BEAR

SMALL AMOUNT OF BLACK MERINO ROVING
FOR GROOM'S BOW TIE

FOUR ⅛" (3 MM) GLASS BLACK EYES

BLACK EMBROIDERY THREAD

35–40 SMALL PEARL SEED BEADS

TWO SIZE 40 OR 42 TRIANGULAR FELTING
NEEDLES AND HOLDER

ONE SIZE 43 TRIANGULAR FELTING NEEDLE
FOR SURFACE FINISHING (OPTIONAL)

FELTING MAT (SPONGE OR BRUSH)

SEWING NEEDLE AND THREAD

TIP

Each bear measures 2¾–3⅛"
(7–8 cm) with a base width of
about 2⅜" (6 cm). You can make
larger bears by increasing the amounts
of wool roving used, but remember to
keep the amounts in proportion.

01 For the main body of the bear, take a 16" (40.5 cm) length of white or cream roving teased out to a strip about 1½" (3.8 cm) wide and fold it over to make a bundle approx 4" x 1½" (10 x 3.8 cm) wide. Take another length of roving approx 12" x 1½" (30.5 x 3.8 cm), fluff it into a loose ball and insert it into one side of the bundle.

02 Pull the outer edges round to enclose the filling and begin working with two needles to form a fat-bottomed bulb with a tapering point. Keep the filling at one end for a base that is wide and flat beneath.

03 As the wool mats together, start pushing one side inward to make a fat, curved teardrop shape. When the body feels quite firm, shape the head, holding the wool in place so that the nose points skyward. Use one needle for precision. You now have your basic bear shape.

04 Take a small amount of roving and, working with one needle, make a stumpy tail on the bear's bottom no more than ⅜" (1 cm) long.

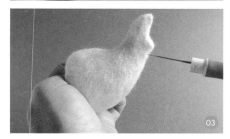

05 Take very small wisps of wool and loosely shape two tiny ears on the felting mat before needling them onto the front of the head.

06 Make the back legs from a length of roving measuring about 6" x 1½" (15 x 3.8 cm) split into two equal parts, shaping each part into a leg by doubling the wool over. When the legs are still soft but nicely

GRETEL PARKER

Children's illustrator Gretel Parker discovered needle felting five years ago. Now her work is collected all over the world and she enjoys passing on her knowledge and spreading the needle felting "bug" to new crafters.
www.gretelparker.com

shaped, attach them to the bottom of the bear in a sitting position. Make the front legs in the same way, but this time use a length of roving approx 4" x 1½" (10 x 3.8 cm), and fix the front legs in between the back legs, pointing them slightly inward. Each leg should be about 2–2⅜" (5–6 cm) when finished, and the thicker tops of the front legs should form the shoulders.

07 Cover the entire body in very thin layers of wool laid in the same direction. Work with one needle (size 43 preferably) for a fine, smooth finish. Sew on the eyes and satin stitch a triangle with black embroidery thread for the nose.

08 To finish the groom, use one felting needle to carefully make a tiny bow tie from a very small wisp of black roving and needle it in place under the bear's chin.

09 Repeat steps 1–7 to make a slightly smaller bear for the bride. Thread the seed beads onto good-quality sewing thread and tie in place around the bride's neck.

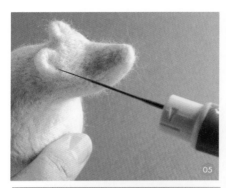

CROCHET LACE
BRIDESMAID'S HAIR ACCESSORY & POSY

MAKE THESE FLOWERBUD HAIR ACCESSORIES, WHICH ARE ABOUT 1½" (3.8 CM) IN DIAMETER, TO MATCH YOUR MAIN COLOR THEME FOR THE BIG DAY. THE DOILY-INSPIRED POSY WRAP, WHICH IS ABOUT 3¾" (9.5 CM) IN DIAMETER, IS WORKED IN ROWS RATHER THAN ROUNDS, GIVING IT AN OPEN SIDE THAT ALLOWS YOU TO WRAP IT AROUND A BOUQUET.

FLORAL
FANCIES

HOW TO MAKE ... BRIDESMAID'S HAIR ACCESSORY & POSY

MATERIALS

ONE 50ɢ BALL (126 YARDS/115 METERS) OF ROWAN COTTON GLACE IN BUBBLES 724 (A), OR SIMILAR YARN (SPORT-WEIGHT COTTON)

ONE 100ɢ BALL (230 YARDS/210 METERS) OF PATONS 100% COTTON DK IN BRIGHT PINK 2725 (B), OR SIMILAR YARN (WORSTED-WEIGHT COTTON YARN)

ONE 50ɢ BALL (227 YARDS/208 METERS) OF ANCHOR ARTISTE BABY SOFT IN CREAM 926 (C), OR SIMILAR YARN (CROCHET COTTON)

SIZE B1 (2 ᴍᴍ) AND SIZE C2 (2.5 ᴍᴍ) CROCHET HOOKS

ONE HAIR CLIP FOR EACH FLOWER-BUD ACCESSORY

ONE SHELL BUTTON AND 40" (101.5 ᴄᴍ) LENGTH OF ⅝" (1.5 ᴄᴍ) WIDE SATIN RIBBON FOR THE POSY WRAP

GLASS-HEADED PINS, SAFETY PIN, AND TAPESTRY NEEDLE

01 Crochet the flower hair accessory. Using yarn A and C2 hook, make 29ch plus 1 tch.

Row 1: 1sc into second ch from hook, 1sc into next ch, *work (1sc, 4ch, 1sc) into next ch, 1sc into next 3ch, rep from * five more times, work (1sc, 4ch, 1sc) into next ch, 1sc into last 2ch, turn.

Row 2: 1ch, skip 3 sts, 7dc into first 4ch loop, miss 2 sts, ss into next st, work [7dc into next 4ch loop, skip 2 sts, ss into next st] twice, *skip 2 sts, 7hdc into next 4ch loop, skip 2 sts, 1sc into next st, rep from * to end, turn.

Fasten off yarn A and join yarn B.

TIP
Experiment with scale by using a smaller hook and finer yarn or a larger hook and thicker yarn.

Row 1

Row 2

01

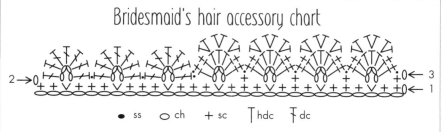

Bridesmaid's hair accessory chart

2→0

1

3

● ss   ○ ch   + sc   ⊤ hdc   ⊤ dc

Row 3: 1ch, ss into first st, *1sc into next 2 sts, 2hdc into next 3 sts, 1sc into next 2 sts, ss into next st, rep from * three more times.
Fasten off yarn, leaving a long enough length to sew the base of the flower.

02 To shape the flowers, sew in all the loose ends except the length left for sewing up. Starting from the smaller single-color petals, roll the flower up, making sure that the chain from the beginning of the pattern almost coils around itself like a spiral. Secure the rolled up flower with a pin. Thread a tapestry needle with the remaining length of yarn ready to finish off the flower securely.

03 Secure the base of the rolled up flower by inserting the needle through all the layers. Repeat this several times, working around the base. Sew in the remaining yarn tail. Stitch the flower to the hair clip.

TIP
This flower-bud design will work perfectly no matter what style of clip, clasp, comb, or grip you choose to use.

TIP
To add some complementary foliage, cut out a simple felt fabric leaf shape and stitch it to the back of the flower.

Abbreviations

(US terms used throughout)
ch: chain
dc: double crochet
dc2tog: double crochet two stitches together (decrease by one)
hdc: half double crochet
MP: make picot
rep: repeat
sc: single crochet
sp: space
ss: slip stitch
st(s): stitch(es)
tch: turning chain
tog: together
US/UK differences:
US sc (single crochet) = UK dc (double crochet)
US hdc (half double crochet) = UK htr (half treble)
US dc (double crochet) = UK tr (treble)

HOW TO MAKE ... POSY (CONTINUED)

TIP

Add beads to the outer edge picots for an extra touch of sparkle.

05 Crochet the bridesmaid's posy wrap. Using yarn C and B1 hook, work 15ch for foundation row plus 3ch (counts as 1dc).

Row 1: 1dc into fourth ch from hook, 1dc into each ch, turn. (16dc)

Row 2: 4ch (counts as 1dc and 1ch), *1dc into next st, 1ch, rep from * 13 times, 1dc into top of 3ch, turn.

Row 3: 5ch (counts as 1dc and 2ch), *1dc into next st, 2ch, rep from * 13 times, 1dc into top of 3ch, turn.

Row 4: Ss into first st and 2ch-sp, 3ch (counts as 1dc), 2dc into same 2ch-sp, *1ch, miss next st, 3dc into next 2ch-sp, rep from * 13 times, turn.

Row 5: Ss into first st, 3ch (counts as 1dc), *work [1dc, 5ch, 1dc] into next st, dc2tog over next 2 sts missing 1ch in between sts, rep from * 13 times, work [1dc, 5ch, 1dc] into next st, 1dc into 3ch, turn.

Row 6: 1ch, ss into first st, *work [2sc, 1hdc, make picot (MP) by working 3ch and ss into top of last st worked, 2dc, MP, 1dc, 1hdc, MP, 2sc] into 5ch loop, ss into top of dc2tog from previous row, rep from * 14 times, working ss into top of 3ch for final repetition. Break yarn and weave in ends.

06 Working on a padded surface, block the crochet using glass-headed pins, making sure to stretch the fabric to open out the design.

07 Place a damp cloth over the top of your pinned-out crochet piece and gently press using a steam iron, then leave to dry thoroughly.

Posy wrap chart

| ● ss | ○ ch | + sc | T hdc | ⊤ dc | ⋁ dc2tog |

08 Sew on the shell button to the fourth row on the wrong side (the button will fasten to the inside of the design). Fasten the button to close the wrap.

09 Take the ribbon and fasten a safety pin to one end of it. This will help you to guide the ribbon as you weave it in and out of the gaps. Tie the ribbon ends in a bow to finish.

CAROL MELDRUM

Carol is a textile designer, author, and workshop tutor based in Glasgow, Scotland, who enjoys nothing better than playing around with yarn, coming up with new ideas, and sharing them with folk at www.beatknit.com and blog.beatknit.com

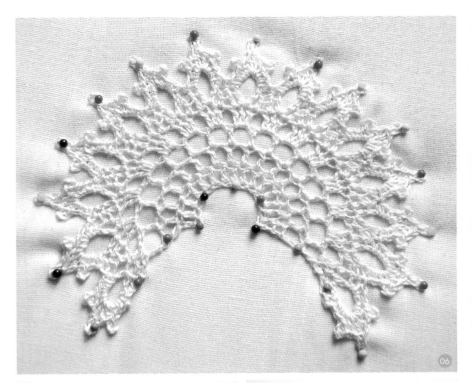

06

08

09

TEMPLATES

ALL THE SHAPES FOR THE BOOK'S MAKES. ENLARGE ALL TEMPLATES BY 200% BY PHOTOCOPYING THE PAGES, WITH THE EXCEPTION OF RING PILLOW AND 3D DIAMOND GARLAND ON PAGE 92, WHICH SHOULD BE ENLARGED BY 400%. YOU CAN ALSO FIND THE FULL-SIZE TEMPLATES READY TO DOWNLOAD FROM WWW.LOVECRAFTS.CO.UK

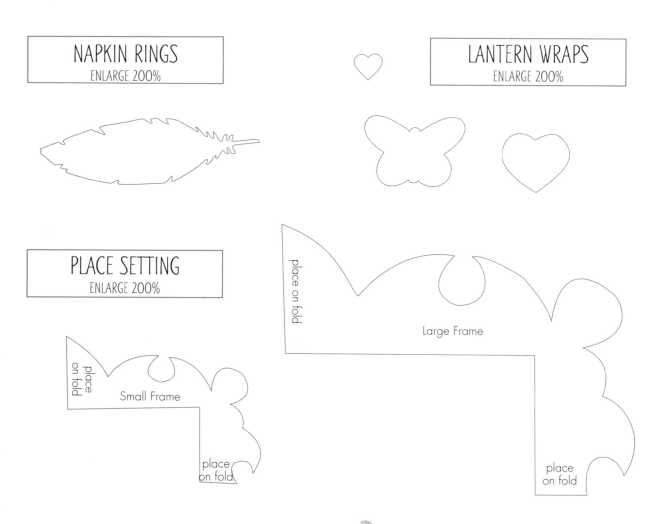

NAPKIN RINGS
ENLARGE 200%

LANTERN WRAPS
ENLARGE 200%

PLACE SETTING
ENLARGE 200%

place on fold

Small Frame

place on fold

place on fold

Large Frame

place on fold

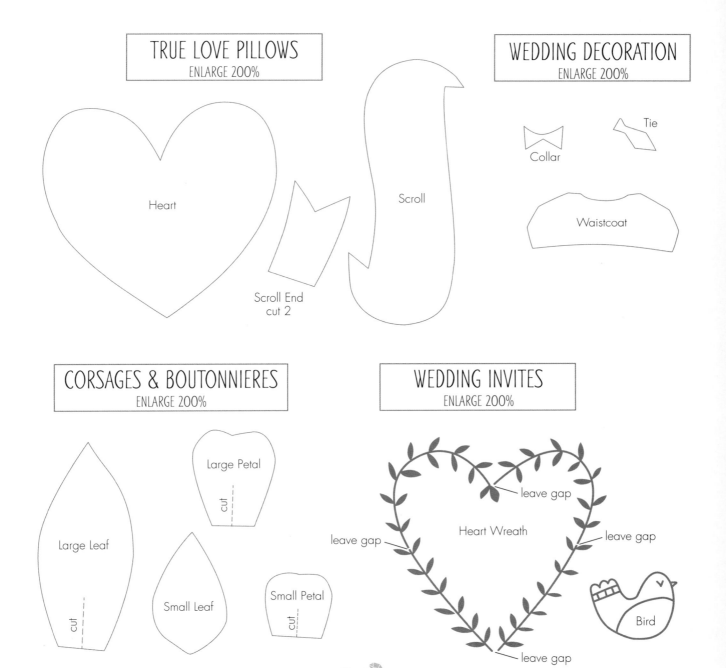

TRUE LOVE PILLOWS
ENLARGE 200%

Heart

Scroll End
cut 2

Scroll

WEDDING DECORATION
ENLARGE 200%

Collar

Tie

Waistcoat

CORSAGES & BOUTONNIERES
ENLARGE 200%

Large Leaf

cut

Large Petal

cut

Small Leaf

Small Petal

cut

WEDDING INVITES
ENLARGE 200%

leave gap

Heart Wreath

leave gap

leave gap

leave gap

Bird

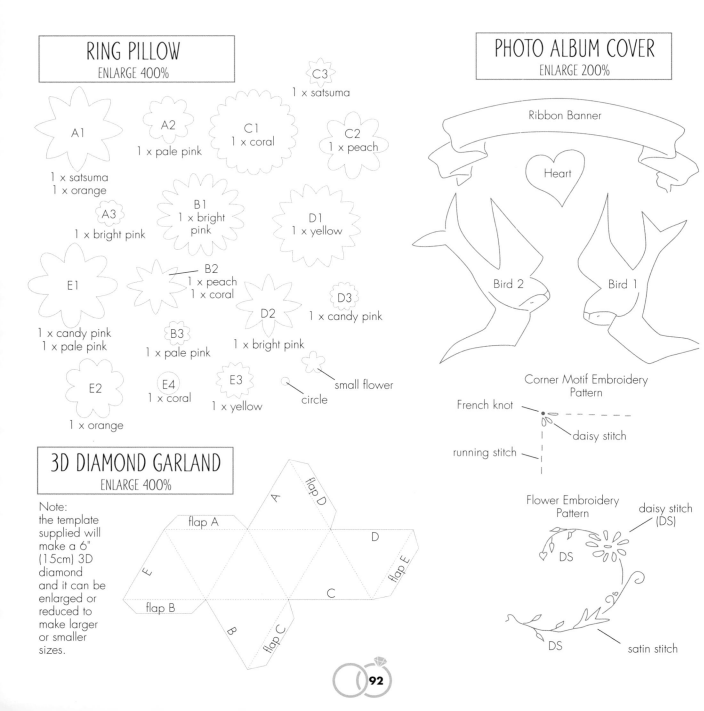

RING PILLOW
ENLARGE 400%

A1
1 x satsuma
1 x orange

A2
1 x pale pink

C1
1 x coral

C3
1 x satsuma

C2
1 x peach

A3
1 x bright pink

B1
1 x bright pink

D1
1 x yellow

E1
1 x candy pink
1 x pale pink

B2
1 x peach
1 x coral

D2
1 x bright pink

D3
1 x candy pink

B3
1 x pale pink

E2
1 x orange

E4
1 x coral

E3
1 x yellow

small flower

circle

3D DIAMOND GARLAND
ENLARGE 400%

Note:
the template supplied will make a 6" (15cm) 3D diamond and it can be enlarged or reduced to make larger or smaller sizes.

flap A
flap D
A
D
E
flap E
flap B
B
C
flap C

PHOTO ALBUM COVER
ENLARGE 200%

Ribbon Banner

Heart

Bird 2

Bird 1

Corner Motif Embroidery Pattern

French knot

daisy stitch

running stitch

Flower Embroidery Pattern

daisy stitch (DS)

DS

DS

satin stitch

GOOD LUCK CHARMS
ENLARGE 200%

Cake

Turtle

Cat

Horseshoe

Heart

WEDDING FAVORS
ENLARGE 200%

Bag

CHARTS

Cross-stitch

Working cross-stitch—method 1
Working left to right, make a row of diagonal stitches. Up at 1, down at 2, up at 3. Repeat. Working right to left, complete the Xs with a row of diagonal stitches. Up at 4, down at 5, up at 6. Repeat.

Working cross-stitch—method 2
Work left to right. Up at 1, down at 2, up at 3. Down at 4, up at 5. Repeat.

Finishing a thread
Slide the needle through five to six stitches on the back of your work to secure and finish off the thread.

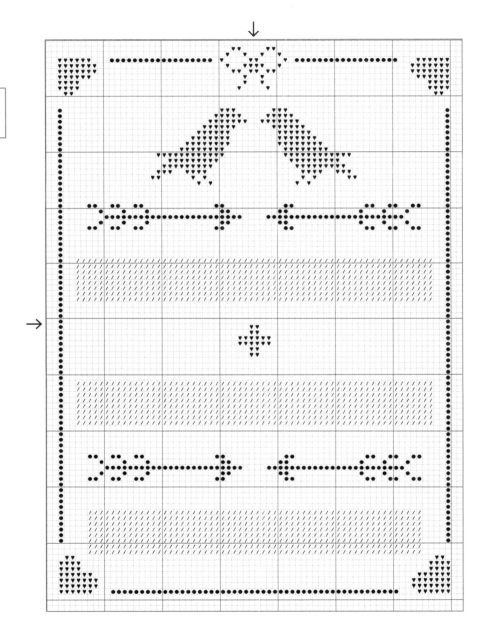

Key

♥ Anchor 926/DMC 712
● Anchor 366/DMC 739

/ Add name/date here

94

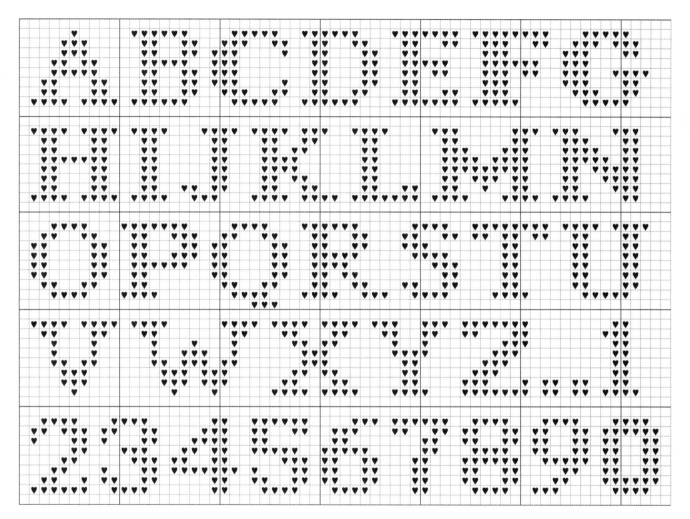

Key

 Anchor 926/DMC 712

DABBLE IN CRAFTY GOODNESS WITH MORE MOLLIE MAKES BOOKS available from Interweave

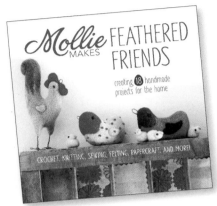

MOLLIE MAKES FEATHERED FRIENDS
Creating 18 Handmade Projects for the Home
ISBN 978-1-59668-775-2 | $12.95

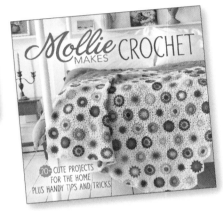

MOLLIE MAKES CROCHET
20+ Cute Projects for the Home
Plus Handy Tips and Tricks
ISBN 978-1-62033-095-1 | $12.95

MOLLIE MAKES WOODLAND FRIENDS
More Handmade Projects for the Home
ISBN 978-1-62033-540-6 | $19.95

For more information
on Mollie Makes
please visit
www.molliemakes.com

First published in the United States in 2013 by
Interweave
A division of F+W Media, Inc.
201 East Fourth Street
Loveland, CO 80537
interweave.com

© 2013 Collins & Brown

ISBN 978-1-62033-541-3

Library of Congress Cataloging-in-Publication Data not available at time of printing.

10 9 8 7 6 5 4 3 2 1

Manufactured in China by 1010.

PUBLISHER'S ACKNOWLEDGMENTS

This book would not have been possible without the input of our crafty contributors, who have provided all our brilliant how-to projects and step-by-step photography. We would also like to thank Cheryl Brown, who has done an excellent job of pulling everything together, and Sophie Martin for her design layout. Thanks to Mollie Johanson for allowing us to use her stitch diagrams. Main project photography by Rachel Whiting.

And of course, thanks must go to the fantastic team at *Mollie Makes* for all their help, in particular Lara Watson, Helena Tracey, Jane Toft, and Katherine Raderecht.